JAPANESE FLOWER ARRANGING
EAST MEETS WEST

With an introduction by Georgie Davidson

**ORBIS BOOKS
LONDON**

Contents

Photographs 1 and 2 are from *Estampes Japonaises* by James A Michiner, Office du Livre, Friburg 1961 (original title *Japanese Prints*, Charles E Tuttle Co, Publishers, Rutland, Vermont and Tokyo 1959); 3 is from *L'art des fleurs au Japon* by Donald Richie, Office du Livre, Friburg 1967 (original title *The Masters' Book of Ikebana*, Bijutsu Shuppan-Sha, Tokyo 1966). Photographs 4, 5, 7 and 58–62 (flower arrangements by the Master Houn Ohara) were taken by Carlo Bevilacqua at an exhibition of Japanese art at the Palazzo del Turismo in Milan; photographs 6 and 8–57 (flower arrangements by Evi Zamperini Pucci) by Marcello Saporetti.

Original drawings in the introduction by Lindsay Pope

From the Italian of Evi Zamperini Pucci

© Istituto Geografico de Agostini, Novara 1972
English edition © Orbis Publishing Limited, London 1973
Phototypeset in England by Petty and Sons Ltd, Leeds
Printed in Italy by IGDA, Novara
ISBN 0 85613 139 3

There are two basic styles which dominate the modern world of flower arrangement: the Japanese or oriental style, and that of the western hemisphere. The fundamental difference between them is that the oriental style is much stronger in line than in colour or mass – perhaps because of the comparative scarcity of decorative plant material in that country, and also because of the worship of simple natural forms which is so innate a part of the Japanese philosophy. The traditional western styles, on the other hand, have undoubtedly benefited by the abundance and variety of plants and flowers in our temperate climate, and are consequently stronger in colour and balanced mass.

In recent years these two styles, so widely divergent in origin, have come to influence each other more and more. The oriental styles have been affected, and to a considerable degree changed, by the influx of western culture and flowers into the east; while at the same time, modern communications and the rapid spread of knowledge have increased our understanding of the east, and removed much of the mystery once associated with all things oriental. Thus we have, in the twentieth century, not only an intermingling of styles, but schools of western-style flower arranging which flourish in the heart of Japan; while more occidentals than ever are qualifying to teach ikebana – oriental flower arranging – in various western countries.

It would be sad indeed if the classical designs of either style disappeared from our modern world, but with the continual breaking down of barriers between countries and races, it is no longer easy – in some cases impossible – to separate the two basic styles distinctly. In this book we have aimed to introduce flower arrangements which are easy for the novice to understand and follow, and have the Japanese simplicity of form which is so popular today. The appreciation of the oriental designs leads us into an understanding of the aspects of Japanese culture and philosophy, to which the different flowers and forms relate. In this respect the book aims to provide an introduction to the more profound, complicated and specialized world of pure ikebana.

As a rule, the materials used in these arrangements are quite common and easily obtainable, and much helpful advice is offered in the extensive text, on the treatment and care of plants. Where more exotic materials have been used, their long life makes this an economical proposition. The choice of container is generally straight-forward; a well-proportioned, simple form is often more valuable than an ornate one. In the slim, controlled Japanese style of flower arrangement, the container plays a more obvious and important part than it would in a western arrangement, where it might be almost obscured by a mass of flowers.

Flowers by their very beauty open many hearts, and the design of flower arrangements is a subject of endless and fascinating discussion. It is perhaps the most transient of all the arts; the flowers are constantly changing, both in their individual form and throughout the seasons; but this is the pleasure and the challenge of using living materials.

The history of flower arranging

In this book our aim is to present simple and modern arrangements of flowers in designs influenced by both occidental and oriental styles. To identify the roots of the art, let us look into the history of the development and designs of flower arranging.

One question often asked in exhibitions of flower arrangements is whether an arrangement is an ikebana (Japanese flower arrangement) or not; the usual answer is 'yes' if it is a line arrangement and 'no' if it is a mass. This is not a good criterion since many of the greatest ikebana masterpieces are mass designs. A great difference is that in ikebana, mass is related to space, and it is a rule that all masses must be well balanced – actually and visually – by aesthetic spaces: the spaces are as important as the masses. In the occidental styles the mass is much more solid and more attention is given to colour than to space. Depth is more often achieved by recession of colours than by direction of line. This has been so from the earliest times; by referring to old prints, paintings and vase decorations in order to draw our comparisons, we find that whereas the oriental flower arrangement was based on the asymmetrical triangle, the occidental favoured a balanced one. Fig. 1 shows an early Japanese arrangement, of about the year 1500. This is an early nageire style, of natural and asymmetric shape – if the line on the left was long the line on the right had to be shorter, and vice versa. This was a period when arrangements were made chiefly to express man's emotions through the medium of living materials. In the western world the pattern and philosophy were not so very different, as you will see in the small detail from the famous Hugo van der Goes altarpiece of about the same time (fig. 2). In this masterpiece the flowers have religious symbolism – the columbines representing the seven gifts of the Holy Spirit, and the dianthus the Virgin's humility. You will note that both containers are simple in the extreme.

From the simple placing of materials in small arrangements a pattern developed in the oriental style which resulted in masterpieces of a quality that could not be achieved without years of study and application. This was the rikkwa, or standing flower arrangement, which put greater emphasis on space (fig. 2a) while including many more lines in the structure. The outline, although still asymmetrical, had to include the main aspects of a general landscape view. The middle and distant mountains, the waterfall and the river, and the village were all incorporated in one magnificent edifice of background, middleground and foreground. This was essentially an arrangement to be seen from three sides, and it broke away from the previous idea, which had been to place the flower arrangement in an alcove (tokonoma – see plate 5 in the colour pages). The materials were kept in position by being pushed into a tight bundle of rice straw. The surface surrounding the stems was covered either with sand or fine stones, which represented the earth from which the landscape arose. Special containers are required for these arrangements for they are, though visually balanced, very small when compared with the

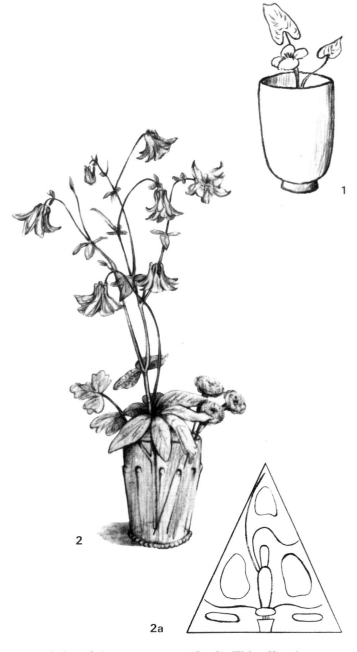

1

2

2a

actual size of the arrangement (fig. 3). This effect is put right by grouping all the stems together for a short distance after they emerge from the opening of the container.

At about this time full and flamboyant styles of flower arranging were being developed in the western hemisphere, as we can see from the drawing (fig. 4) taken from a painting by the artist Roelandt Savery (1576–1639), the original of which can be seen in a museum in Utrecht. One has to acknowledge the artist's licence with these paintings, for although nowadays, with sophisticated world transport methods, the seasons of flowers are no longer clearly defined – we have daffodils at Christmas and chrysanthemums all the year round – this was not so in the sixteenth century. The beautiful paintings of the time were influenced not only by the seasons and the religious ideas of the artists but also by the fashion of the period.

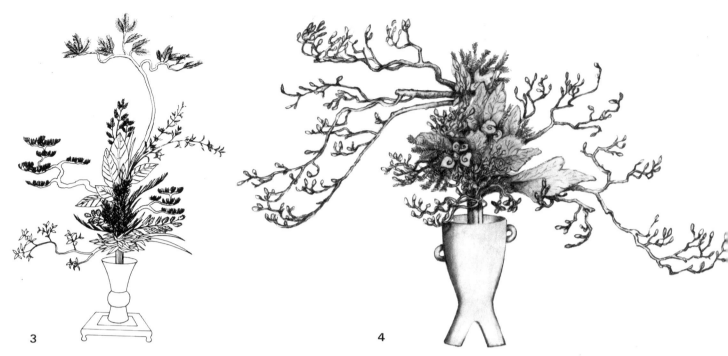

3

4

New design trends

Fig. 5 shows a rikkwa composition of a much later era
which retains the form typical of the style and yet is
quite modern. The creation is representative of the new
trend in the rikkwa of the oldest classical school of
ikebana in Japan – the Ikenobo. The teaching of this
school has upheld the classical traditions of ikebana and is
still the leader in this field. The centrally-grouped stems
are an integral part of all traditional arrangements of the
school. When it became evident, with the spread of
interest in the art, that the large set pieces were too
complicated for the general enthusiast to make, the
school created a new and smaller style called shoka which
was within the scope of all pupils provided they had the
diligence to study. This style, composed of three lines
(fig. 6) retains the central balance and grouped stems of its
forebears and has an elegance of its own. In both the
shoka and the rikkwa styles the stems go right to the
bottom of the container. In the smaller shoka form they
are kept in position by a forked kubari.

In fig. 7 we see a typical triangular arrangement with
the looser mass of the western style. You will see that the
sides are carefully balanced and that the central flower is
the longest. This downward-curving arrangement was
designed to stand on a pedestal. The fixing medium could
be either crushed wire netting or oasis. The outline
instruction for such a design suggests that the central
line is placed first, as it is the longest and governs the
design. The drooping side lines should be placed next,
inserted carefully to ensure that the stems are able to
drink the water. Colour shading is perhaps more
important than form in such styles.

Moon arrangements are very popular in the Japanese
schools of flower arranging, and they are widely used
in western homes. Fig. 8 illustrates one from the classical
era of ikebana, and one from the present day is shown
in fig. 9. You will notice that in the classical style the

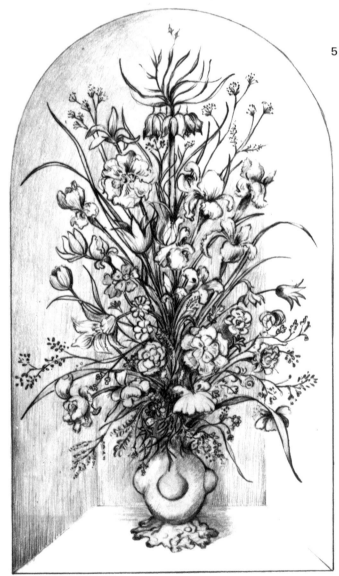

5

grouped stems are at an angle and not vertical as in the shoka and rikkwa styles. This adds considerably to the flow of the lines. One has the choice, when using moon-shaped containers, of interpreting a waxing, a waning, or a full, moon. In the classical arrangement, because the lines are flowing to the left, it is accepted that the moon is waxing. In the modern style arrangement the moon, because the longest line is falling and to the right, is on the wane. Fig. 10 shows a diagram of the classical form. A full moon also has three main lines, a long one in the centre and a shorter one on either side of it, within the circle of the container (fig. 11). In the modern styles the outline remains as in the classical form but stems at the base are not grouped as one.

With the introduction of many types of western flowers to their country, the Japanese schools of flower arranging and their masters had to modify their designs to accommodate the new materials. The old nageire style was one of the first to be redesigned and this proved to be very popular, for it kept to a large extent the natural placing and simple combination of the materials, but allowed much more freedom than the somewhat formal and rigid shoka and rikkwa styles (fig. 12). As taller vases came into use it was no longer practical for the stems to reach the bottom of them, and so the matagi kubari – the fixing which had kept the shoka lines in position – had to be modified. The Sogetsu school, among others, designed several alternative ways of fixing materials into position in these tall containers (fig. 13). The purpose of these kubaris is to keep the materials balanced and in position: for this balance it is not necessary to use thick sticks – well-fitting slender ones will offer an equal amount of support. The weight displacement of the branch tells the arranger at which point the greatest support will be required. In ikebana it cannot be stressed too strongly that the kubari is chosen to balance the branch, and therefore it should not be selected until after the weight distribution of the branch is understood. When these tall containers are used for the full western style of arrangement, oasis or wire can be packed into them. The great difference between the two styles is that the oriental uses only one quarter of the neck opening of the container (whereas the western style uses it all); branches emerge from the container at the correct angle to make a good line. Branches may have to be reshaped: do this by bending, twisting or by partially cutting and wedging them.

The tea ceremony

Chabana arrangements, which fall into the old nageire category, are never composed independently of their background. These exquisitely simple forms are called chabana because of their use at the tea ceremony. Because of the nature of the ceremony and the austerity of the surroundings, the choice of materials must be at one

6

7

8

9

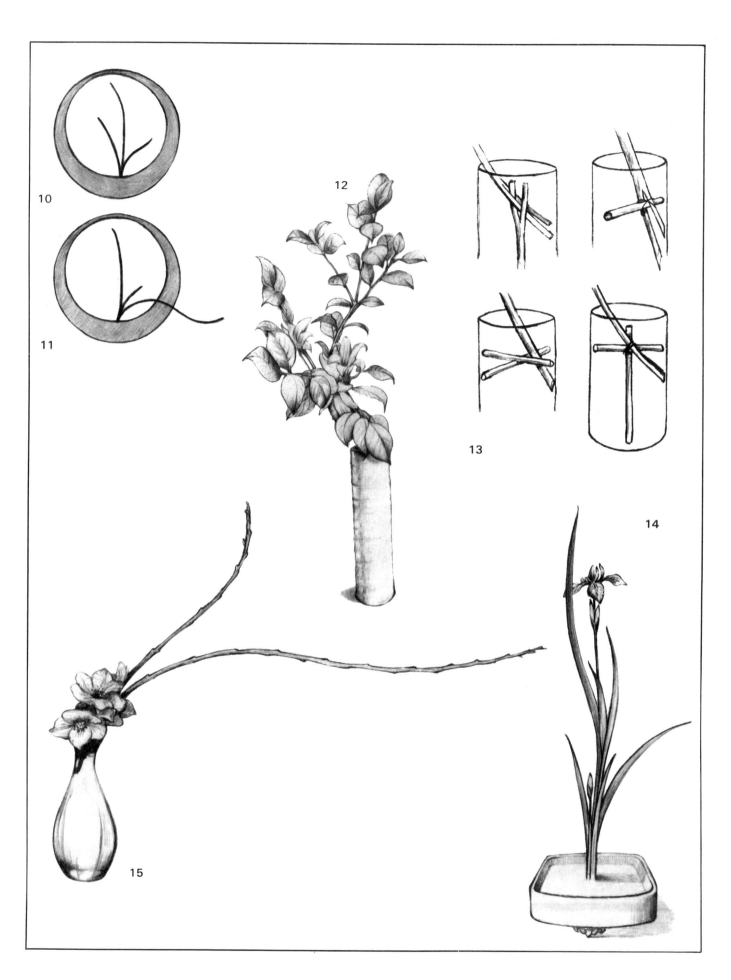

10

11

12

13

14

15

with the mood of the tea master, the colour and form of the implements used, and the arrangement must be correctly placed for the source of light. This is one of the most difficult ikebana arrangements to master, for one needs to create an impression of size with a minimum of material, and the finished work should be equal to the occasion but must not dominate it. The Japanese name for this style is wabi (quiet taste), and the nearest western equivalent is the specimen glass in which we rather casually place a single flower. We are careful in choosing the bloom but rather rely on its isolated beauty for its effect. The illustrations show: fig. 14, chabana of the Ikenobo school; fig. 15, a modern interpretation of the old style; and fig. 16, a simple placement of a single flower.

From flower arrangements for the tea ceremony it is a natural progression to arrangements for the table, and here we have to rely on the modern schools of both oriental and occidental styles for designs, and for earlier examples and history on the glossy pages of Mrs Beeton's or other cookery and household management books. The Japanese keep the asymmetrical triangle as the foundation of their designs; the diagrams show arrangements from the Sogetsu school, possibly the most modern of all schools of ikebana in Japan. The circle round the pinholder is divided into three unequal segments by three main lines (fig. 17). These spaces are then filled in with short pieces of foliage and/or flowers (fig. 17a). The pinholder is placed to one side of the container and the longer lines are placed so that they cross the wider sections of it.

Table arrangements

The most favoured western arrangement for the dining table is a carefully balanced design with a central spine running the length of it (fig. 18). The fixing medium is placed in the centre and all lines radiate from it. The order of placement recommended is first, centre; second, the ends – and third the sides (fig. 18a). Then fill in. Our Victorian ancestors have left us quite a legacy of designs,

16

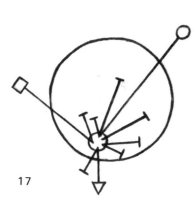

17

17a

9

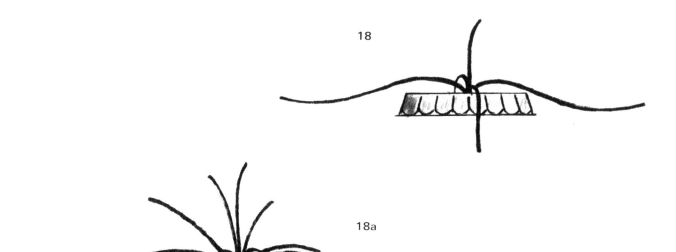

18

18a

including that illustrated in fig. 19, using fruit with leaves. The delicacy of this arrangement contrasts startlingly with the rather severe modern version of the same design (fig. 20).

Your china and table accessories, and the occasion, should influence your table flower design. Since these styles are placed in shallow water, good conditioning of the materials will play a great part in their success – for no matter how well the arrangement looks at the beginning of dinner, if it is flagging by the end of the evening the first good impression will be forgotten and the whole effect of your work spoiled. There are many products available in the shops which are said to help flowers to last longer, but the oldest remedy of all is a perfectly safe one and hard to beat: first give the materials a good soak in deep water, and then make the last cut in the stems under water before arranging. Of course containers and fixing mediums should be clean and knives or cutting shears sharp. The removal of all leaves below the water line also helps to keep the water fresh.

From the arrangements of the Renaissance and the formal rikkwa designs of the east, flower arrangers have come a long way to arrive at the flat containers and informal designs which are so popular today (fig. 21). The two sources have blended, separated and come together again – in traditional designs both east and west retain their individuality, but in the modern arrangements it is sometimes difficult to tell which is which, such has been the influence of the one on the other.

Making modern designs

To the general public, an arrangement in the Japanese style often seems modern – especially when contrasted with the traditional arrangements of the western world. To the ikebana enthusiast, however, a modern arrangement is one in which the materials have been

19

used for their shape, colour and texture, and not for their natural beauty. There is a planned approach to this – the first exercise is to construct asymmetrical triangles with three lines of different lengths and different materials. These are made into a variety of patterns, each of which enables the arranger to bring out the individual beauty of the material by emphasizing the space around it. Depth and balance are achieved by designing into each arrangement three triangles, two scalene and one equilateral. One of these is outlined by drawing a line from the tip of one branch to another when taking the elevation view (fig. 22). The second is outlined when drawing a similar line when taking a plan view (fig. 23). The first is used to correct the angle, and the second the position. The equilateral triangle is made by the main line materials on the pinholder. When we have learnt to compose different and slightly unnatural patterns (so far as the growing habits of the materials go), and to see our materials as colours and shapes rather than as natural blooms; when we can assess the possibilities of the materials, design for certain given positions and construct with enough assurance and technique to carry

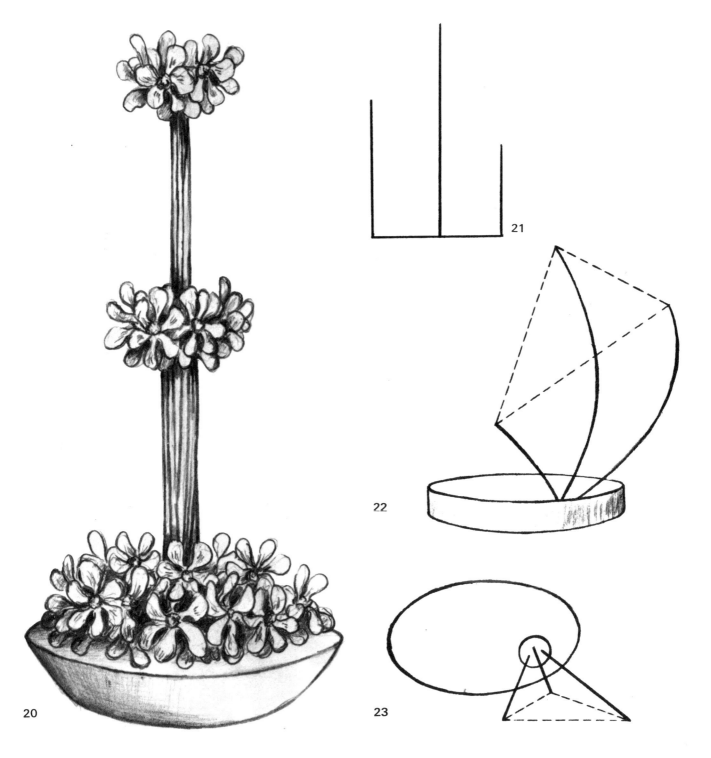

20

21

22

23

11

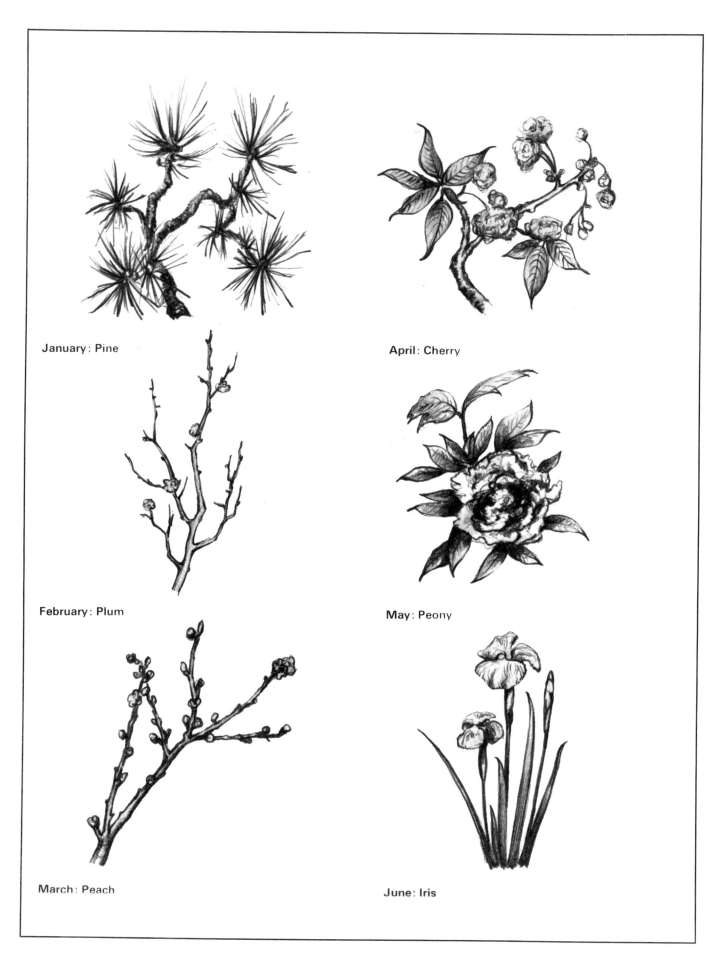

January: Pine

February: Plum

March: Peach

April: Cherry

May: Peony

June: Iris

out our intended design – then we may confidently venture into the modern field of arranging.

The western forms of arrangement also have their rules, and advice is given on the length of the stems and proportion between the container and the material. Most of the shapes are solid, the globe and the pyramid being two of the favourites. A halved globe is often used for pedestals, and then flowing tendrils are allowed to soften the 'cut edge'.

As messages are often expressed by the materials in oriental flower arrangements, and as the arrangements in this book are oriental, strongly influenced by the west, you may find it interesting to know the meanings of the plants which are the accepted symbols of the calendar months of the year.

January: Pine

Pine is one of the 'three friends of winter', used in arrangements made for the New Year. The other 'friends' are bamboo and flowering plum. Pine, considered the king of trees, symbolizes long life, courage and endurance, because it is evergreen; it can grow in a crevice on a bleak mountainside, and it is a particularly strong and long-living tree. Some of Japan's most treasured trees of this species are over seven hundred years old. Their long life and beauty is undoubtedly the result of the great care and attention lavished on them, for their lovely lines are not entirely nature's work but largely the result of years of careful pruning and training. Different types of pine have different numbers of needles in each group. The twin-needle pine, in particular, is used to convey special wishes on the occasion of a marriage.

February: Plum

Plum blossom, one of the 'three friends of winter', is not the cultivated type, which bears the sweet fruit we know in the west; it is the wilder variety, the fruits of which are inedible. It is one of the first trees to flower in the New Year, and so it ends the dreariness of winter. It symbolizes beauty, virtue and nobility. The blossom is highly valued for its fragrance. Branches of plum are often used as subjects in old prints and hanging scrolls, because with age they become gnarled, twisted, moss-covered and very beautiful. Old branches are saved and used again and again with other materials.

March: Peach

The peach blossom is associated with femininity. It symbolizes perfection, and is adored for its very soft and delicate flowers. It is the traditional flower used for the Girls' Festival, and should be used in its natural state, not twisted and shaped. Small arrangements of peach branches are made to stand on the lower steps of a stand, made especially to hold the dolls displayed at this time. It is often combined with the yellow flowers of wild mustard for this festival. The arrangement conveys a wish for all the feminine attributes of gentleness, beauty and happiness for the daughters of the house. Many weddings take place during this month, when the blossom is at its most attractive stage.

April: Cherry

The cherry blossom symbolizes perfection and is worshipped and glorified as is no other tree in Japan. The whole nation celebrates when the cherry trees bloom, and hundreds of poems have been written about cherry blossom; it is the national flower of Japan. The blossoms are rarely used in flower arrangements for they fall quickly, and this could introduce a note of sadness. If used they are combined with evergreens and not with other flowering materials, since their beauty is considered to be too pure to mix with anything else. The trees are not of the fruit-producing variety, but the blossom is sometimes collected to make tea.

May: Peony

The peony stands for shyness and prosperity, because its bud is slow to open and the flower retains its beauty for such a long time. In China the peony is considered the king of all the flowers. In Japan it is also highly thought of, and is one of the three flowers accorded royal rank. The herbaceous and the tree peony are so similar that they are referred to as 'twin sister flowers'. When using them in arrangements it is usual to have one fully-opened bloom amid buds and half-opened flowers. They are usually arranged alone rather than with other plants.

June: Iris

Included in the Iris family are flowers with both male and female attributes. It is however the *Iris ensata* which is most famous in Japan; it is the flower used for the Boys' Festival, because the narrow swordlike leaves symbolize courage, the tall straight stems denote uprightness, and the mauve and white flowers nobility. The *Iris sanguinea* (Siberian Flag) is considered to be feminine. Many arrangements are made with iris flowers, and when they are available the leaves are used as abundantly. One of the most popular arrangements in the west and one which is always considered to be very oriental, is that in which irises and their leaves are placed in graduated groups in a large shallow container. The fixing media, usually pinholders, are covered with small, smooth-worn stones and polished pebbles to increase the impression of a water garden.

July: Morning Glory

The short-lived flower of one of the most prolific flowering plants is called 'the poor man's flower'. The Japanese are very enthusiastic about this plant, and many large and beautiful varieties have been developed. The blooms last a little longer if cut before the sun reaches them, and they are usually arranged alone. The morning glory symbolizes affection and attachment. An old legend tells of a man cutting down all but one of the morning glory plants in his garden so that the beauty of a single flower could be seen in solitary splendour from the tokonoma in the tea house.

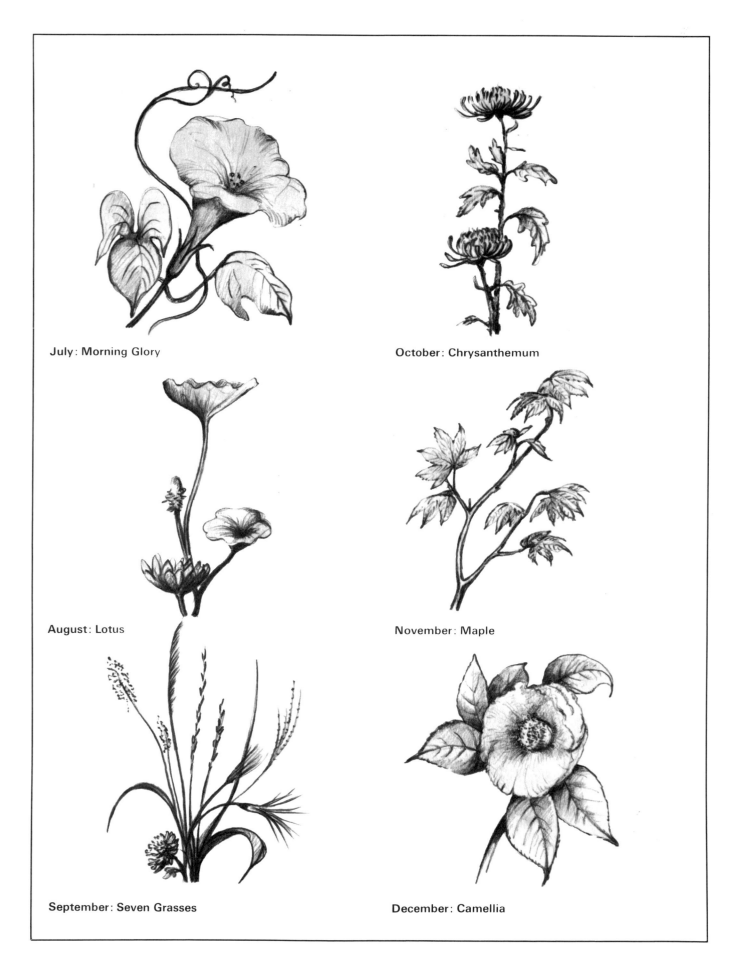

July: Morning Glory

October: Chrysanthemum

August: Lotus

November: Maple

September: Seven Grasses

December: Camellia

August: Lotus

The lotus plant is closely associated with Buddhism, and ceremonial arrangements for the temples were often made from its flowers and leaves. One of the first rikkwa arrangements, in which only one type of material was allowed, was made with lotus flowers and leaves. The phases of existence were expressed by using its seed heads, open and furled leaves, and open flowers and buds. In Japan people gather in parties to view the flowers, which open before dawn and close when the sun rises. The dried seed pods are very popular in arrangements of dried materials; they can also be used at Christmas, when the holes in them can be filled with brightly coloured beads to make an attractive decoration.

September: Seven Grasses

This collection of grasses symbolizes the coming of autumn. They appear in many Japanese paintings and have been the inspiration of many poems. A festival held on the seventh day on the seventh month is called the Festival of Nanakusa. The grasses are gathered at this time, on what would usually be the last country walk before autumn sets in. In Japan, flower arrangement materials are divided into trees and grasses – therefore anything that is not a tree is a grass, and flowers are included in the grasses. The usual collection of grasses would include clover, pampas, vine, pink, patrina, thoroughwort and bellflower.

October: Chrysanthemum

The chrysanthemum is the emblem of the Imperial court of Japan and symbolizes peace, nobility and long life. The Japanese have applied a great deal of horticultural skill to the development of this plant since it was introduced into their country from China, in the eighth century. It is said that there are now more than five thousand varieties in existence. The leaves are often almost as beautiful as the blooms, and should be handled with care, for they are just as easily damaged. If some petals should fall, drop white candle wax in the space to prevent other petals from falling. Chrysanthemums last longer if the stems are broken under water than if they are cut. They should be stood in at least six inches of water overnight to harden.

November: Maple

The message of the maple is 'faithful to the end'. The leaves have to be drastically thinned to bring out the beauty of the line of the branch. As some varieties soften very quickly, it helps if you harden them for twelve hours in salted water (one tablespoon of salt to a quart of water). The leaves will benefit from an occasional spray with clear water. The lovely autumn tints of these leaves can be captured for winter use if the leaves are dried in one of the new crystal mixtures – one or two days is usually long enough for this. When dried, the leaves are so light that they can be glued back into position on their original branches.

December: Camellia

The camellia is the emblem of pride, contentment and domesticity. It is undoubtedly a plant of exquisite beauty, but until recent varieties were bred to overcome its sad habit of dropping its blooms, it had to be avoided, for the falling bloom could be taken as an omen of fall in prestige, or even of sudden death. The leaves can be wiped with milk to retain their polished look. If you are stripping the leaves to obtain a line, remember that a leaf is necessary to draw the water up to the flowers, so leave one just below them. Single flowers are often used in chabana arrangements. Cut branches will keep for months if left standing in water in a cool, dark place.

Bibliography

Allen, Ellen Gordon *Japanese Flower Arranging – a complete primer*, Tuttle, Rutland, USA 1963

Carr, Rachel – *Stepping Stones to Japanese Floral Art*, McKay, New York 1959

Davidson, Georgie – *Classical Ikebana*, W H Allen, London and A S Barnes, New Jersey 1970

Davidson, Georgie – *Ikebana*, W H Allen, London, and A S Barnes, New Jersey 1967

Ikenobo Sen'ei – *Ikenobo School*, Shufunotomo-sha, Tokyo 1961

Ohara, Houn – *Ohara School*, Shufunotomo-sha, Tokyo 1962

Ritchie, Donald, and Weatherby, Meredith – *The Masters' Book of Ikebana*, Thames & Hudson, London 1966

Sparnon, Norman – *Japanese Flower Arrangement*, Tuttle, Rutland, USA 1960

Teshigahara, Kasumi – *Space and Colour in Japanese Flower Arranging*, Kodansha, Tokyo 1965

Teshigahara, Sofu – *Sogetsu School*, Sufunotomo-sha, Tokyo 1962

Wood, Mary Cokely – *Flower Arranging Art of Japan*, Tuttle, Rutland, USA 1952

3 The rikkwa (standing flower) arrangement illustrated here is a particularly interesting one in that balance is maintained between large and slender leaves. The arranger has skilfully combined a variety of materials, bringing out the individual beauty of each yet making a representative whole. The use of the long slender leaves on the left as a counter-balance to the rather short, though flowing, spray at the bottom right-hand side is surely the stroke of a master arranger. The illustration is in fact part of a series published in 1673. The outline and form of these 'standing flower' arrangements was rigidly disciplined, but nevertheless the brilliance of the individual masters shone through. Three planes, the distant, the middle and the foreground are clearly seen in this masterpiece. A 'water lifting' technique had to be used to achieve some of the angles and to feed the shorter-stemmed materials. In large modern occidental arrangements this technique is also followed and water is 'lifted' by means of metal cones. In the old rikkwa arrangements pieces of bamboo were used – the bamboo plant tends to seal itself off in sections, so providing natural 'cones'. The bamboo has another great asset in that it is very strong, and so a large portion below the 'cone' could be cut away without destroying the support required to hold a water section in position. As well as water lifting, these large arrangements often required carpentry; with such angles to follow it was often difficult to get branches which complied naturally.

1 The print on the previous page is by the famous artist Isoda Koryusai, most of whose masterpieces were created between the years 1760 and 1780. These great works are on the themes of art, poetry and love, and reflect the aristocratic atmosphere of ancient Japan. In the first print of this book the lovely Michinoku is seen reading some love poems while two of her maidens are immersed in a game of cards – the cards show that the game is based on a profound knowledge of famous lyrics. An apparently simple floral composition completes the picture in order to show the high cultural level of Japanese ladies of that period. During this time – the second half of the eighteenth century – ikebana arrangements were made according to very strict rules, and knowledge of it was assiduously acquired. Some of the greatest masters of the art at that time taught that man could only find happiness by living in perfect harmony with nature, particularly by following 'kado' – the 'path of flowers' – and that the technique of flower arrangement must be followed if one were to find the much-sought inner peace and spiritual balance necessary for a true communion between man and the marvellous world of nature. This teaching, combined with the philosophical principles taught by the Buddhist monks who came to Japan in the eighteenth century, was welcomed by the aristocratic classes and gradually became accepted by the people as a whole. Japan, as a Shinto country, glorified nature and so was particularly receptive to these ideas. The extent to which the people of Japan were able to absorb these principles is shown in the ikebana, the gardens, the painting and in one of the ceremonies for which they are most famous – the chan no yu (tea ceremony).

2 In the second print, of the same era and still in the ancient tradition, by another great artist Chobunsai Eishi, a young girl has just taken a precious doll from its box, and is about to place it in position in preparation for the traditional Hinamatsuri Festival. This festival, held annually on the third day of the third month, is known as the Girls' Festival or the Festival of Dolls. At this time the flowering peach trees are normally at their best. These blossoms with their delicate beauty are regarded as portraying feminine grace, and, by the shortness of their life, the transitory miracle of youth. The collection of dolls is placed on ceremonial steps, which are covered in red for the occasion. A full set, normally collected over the years and regarded as heirlooms, consists of about fifteen dolls. The most important pair, the Emperor and the Empress, are placed on the top step; they are the most gorgeously robed figures in the collection. Placed on the lower steps in strict order of precedence are the Ladies of the Court, Ministers and High Officials; and then a selection of household articles. On the lowest step a simple but carefully executed arrangement of peach blossom is placed.

18

4–5 The tea house and the tokonoma not only became part of the way of life in Japan, but part of the architecture as well. These photographs show examples, built for an exhibition, of these two important features. They are not always shown in such proximity. The tokonoma (alcove) is built as part of the tea house, but for those who could not afford this luxury, it became an adjunct to the main living room of the dwelling house. The original tokonoma consisted of two alcoves separated by a solid screen – one was fitted with shelves and the other had a raised floor. The latter section was used for displaying one or two highly prized articles, such as an incense burner, a scroll and a flower arrangement. The tokonoma was situated in such a way as to allow the light to filter through the outer side of the higher-floored recess, and so one finds that sometimes this recess is on the right and sometimes on the left. This seemingly minor point is a very important one to the arranger of the flowers to be placed in this tokonoma, for rules governing the in and yo (light and dark) sides of the work had to be strictly adhered to. In most of the tokonomas now constructed, especially in the western world, the shelved section is omitted and a simple alcove in which a scroll (kakemono) and a flower arrangement is placed has now been accepted. It is as well to know, however, that it was originally a two-sectioned affair. The original purpose of it was not only to have a space in which to display treasures and works of art but, far more important, to have a space before which one could sit and gaze and, through its quietness and austerity, gain the peace needed for meditation. The tea house itself is a separate building quite apart from the main dwelling, consisting of an anteroom; a small room for storing the utensils used during the ceremony; a waiting room – through which one entered the main room; and the main room itself. The size of the main tea room is governed by the number of tatami mats used to cover the floor – the orthodox number being four and a half. Not more than five people normally attend the informal ceremony at one time, and it can last for five hours. The formal ceremony is a rarity even in Japan, and is almost unknown in the west. Strict discipline is observed throughout both of these ritualistic ceremonies.

The tea ceremony (chan no yu) cult produced many teachers, some of whom rose to be eminent masters of the art and were honoured men in Japan. It is not possible to be a general student of the art, for the ritual differs not only from one master to another, and one ceremony to another, but from one type of tea to another. As well as philosophy and discipline the ceremony places great emphasis on esoteric values and so the articles used have to be of the finest workmanship. Some of the most beautiful of Japanese ceramics have been made for it, and other special utensils and containers are traditionally used.

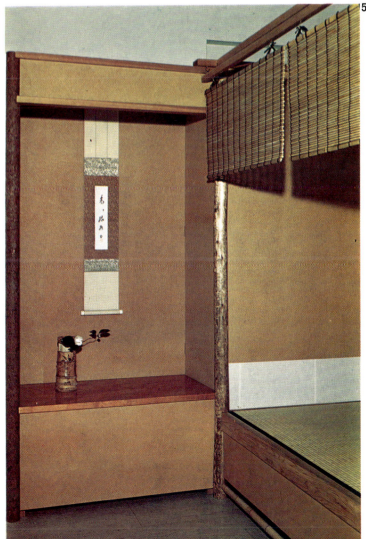

6

7 This is a close-up of the arrangement shown on the previous page in the tokonoma, which illustrates how very beautiful one small flower and a few leaves can be. This arrangement is typical of the style which is made for the tea ceremony and so has been given the special name of chabana.

6 The containers used for flower arranging in general, and ikebana in particular, vary with the season of the year and with the style of arrangement required. The Japanese are perhaps stricter about this than the occidentals – they say, for instance, that some should be put on bases and that some should not. Some folk tales, handed down through the generations, indicate how some of the rather more abstruse rulings came into being. For instance, the container on the left of the photograph is a descendant of the 'well bucket' and the story stems from an incident when a famous tea master was crossing a bridge, from the parapet of which a priest was filling his water buckets. The priest cut the rope joining the buckets to offer water to the master. That is why you may see, some hundreds of years later, a rope coiled around the base of a bucket in which there is a flower arrangement. When two bucket-shaped containers are used together they are never placed at the same level – one always stands, or is hung, higher than the other.

The next two containers shown are natural ones cut from between the nodes of a large bamboo. An advantage of this type of container is that although you have good height, the actual inside depth is only half the height, and less of the stem is hidden. This type of container is especially valuable to students of the classical schools of Japanese flower arranging which require the stems actually to touch the bottom of the containers.

The large container on the right has two openings in which arrangements can be made; often branch material is placed in one and flowers in the other. These are known as the cliff climbing and the cliff hanging arrangements; in the first, small flowers bloom at the top of the cliff and the tree material grows up from the bottom to shelter them, and in the second the reverse happens. The larger woven container on the wall is a copy of an old-style fishing basket, and can be used in both the hanging and the horizontal positions. The smaller bottle-shaped basket is suitable for chabana style arrangements. Both have bamboo or simulated bamboo linings. Bamboo has a tendency to crack when subjected to central heating or excessive drying out. To the Japanese this presents no difficulty for they interpret the split as signifying age, and, as age is to be venerated, they place the split to the front. Quite a lot of advice is offered as to how to prevent the bamboo from splitting. Some people recommend keeping the containers in a refrigerator; others use crystals to keep them dry, and still others keep them wet. There is not, to my knowledge, a guaranteed formula, but it certainly seems that excessive dryness is the cause of most damage.

20

8

8 This is an arrangement typical of the east/west style which is developing and becoming popular; it has a close affinity with both styles. The container is of a style widely used for occidental work, and the centrally placed arrangement also follows this school. The oriental influence is seen in the line and the controlled mass. The materials have been placed in a well pinholder which has been concealed with sunflower seeds. Pinholders usually need to be covered, for they are not the most beautiful things to behold; boxes of stones in various sizes are sold especially for this. In larger containers pieces of rock, root and even coral are brought into use. If you dislike these additions, or they spoil the balance or detract from your arrangement, try placing a leaf in a low forward position, over the front edge of the container if possible, and you will be pleasantly surprised to see how much of the offending kenzan disappears from view.

The stems of grevillia are often too hard and thin to be impaled with any security on a pinholder. To overcome this, the grevillia is placed in a short length of hollow stem, thick enough to grip the pins. This addition of a false stem stub is often necessary with sweet peas, freesias, miniature roses, asparagus fern and other thin-stemmed materials. The mat on which the finished arrangement is standing is of a popular type made from slices of bamboo glued together. Both the grevillia and the marigolds are good materials for drying, and this arrangement could be an all-the-year-round one. Both materials will dry by being hung upside down in a dark, airy place, but the flowers will have a better colour if they are immersed in dry sand for seven to fourteen days. Care should be taken not to flatten the petals during the covering process. Remember also that dried petals are more easily broken than fresh ones.

9

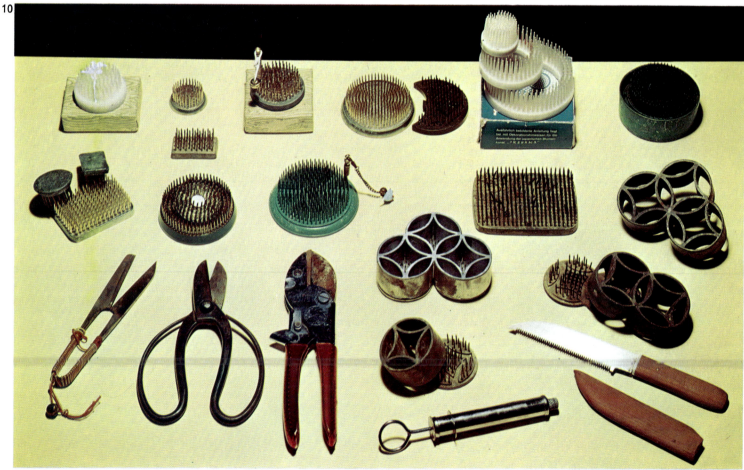

10

9, 11–12 Many containers are made of split bamboo and rattan. These materials are woven into both plain and intricate patterns and a great variety of shapes. The special ones made by individual artists have, on one of the slats, the signature of the artist. In the past these containers were used only during the summer months with light materials and grasses, but nowadays the use is much more general, and, as we can see in the arrangements made in plain baskets in **11** and **12**, heavier materials and bright colours can be made to look gay in them.

10 The equipment of the arranger of flowers, whether in the style of the east or the west, has become both varied and sophisticated as the enthusiasm for the art has grown. One piece in particular merits mention. Whereas in the past one had to master the often difficult problems of fixing the materials so that they would stay in position, now we have a really magnificent aid – known to some Europeans as a pinholder, to others as a kaffir bed, in the USA as a pricker, and to orientals as a kenzan. This was the invention of a Japanese flower master who was the head of the Ohara school of ikebana. Up to the time of this invention the shippo – shown on the right of the picture – had been used for arrangements made in shallow vessels. The most recent advance has been to model a pinholder to fit into the base of the shippo, since in this way greater weight at the base is gained. As the pinholder became popular in the west, where the style of arranging required a firmer fixing, lighter types were made, such as those shown, with plastic pins. These are stuck into position. Pinholders now are so generally used that all shapes and sizes are obtainable. Invaluable to the user of the metal-pinned type is the little straightener. This has a hollow end for sliding over pins to bring them back into position, and often unscrews in the middle to reveal a small nail which is used for removing the little bits of débris which invariably become wedged between the pins. Various knives, saws, syringes are offered as aids. Some of them are good working tools and some are merely playthings – your own judgement must guide you, for there are far too many to enumerate here. Flower shears have perhaps received as much attention as anything from manufacturers, and we have a great variety to choose from, which fall mostly into two categories – those with springs and those without. Those with are excellent for cutting heavy materials but are tiring to hold, and those without are a pleasure to hold but more awkward if one is cutting heavy materials. The small bell or charm is usually attached to the end of the straightener – this makes it easy to find among the stems and general rubbish with which the arranger is often surrounded, since the rule that 'cleanliness is next to godliness' is unfortunately not as rigidly adhered to as it might be.

11

12

13

13 The baskets made especially for flower arranging are usually fitted with liners, made either from natural or simulated bamboo. Many dual purpose baskets available nowadays do not have them, and it is therefore a good idea to keep a variety of shallow pinholder cups available. The baskets are of course light-weight and not always flat at the base, so small heavy glass dishes are most practical. The arrangement shown on the left is clearly reminiscent of the 'heavenly' style in the Ohara school of ikebana. This is a modern school specializing in natural style and landscape arrangements. The exaggerated line of the vine takes the arrangement away from the triangular style of the occidental arranger, and gives it a freedom and gaiety of its own. The colour combination of red and white is used in the orient for special and festive occasions. Both materials used in this arrangement, the roses and the lilacs, have a tendency to droop, and so require special care. The roses will benefit by being cut under water two or three times, totally immersed for about thirty minutes and then left in five inches of water overnight. After they are arranged, spray them occasionally with water. Lilac needs to have the lower

leaves removed, its stems crushed at the base and to be given four or five hours in deep water prior to arranging. It also likes to be sprayed occasionally. Oasis can of course be used instead of a pinholder for fixing this style of arrangement which is full at the base, but there will be a tendency for it to tip over.

14 Arrangements made in tall vases similar to those shown above have a lightness and character which is not possible to achieve in the larger flat types. The centre of the design is so much higher that there is a different point of balance. In the narrow-necked bottles oasis tends to slip down, so unless you have some small mesh bags in which to hold it, it is better to use a roll of wire.

15 Bases are sometimes used to enhance the colour or line of the arrangement or to give balance. These are available in a variety of shapes and colours; often one side is dark and the other bright. Small stones, rocks, roots, pieces of coral are all useful as obscurers of pinholders. Wires and picks are indispensable aids when using dried materials.

16

16 Plastic-covered wire mesh is placed as a fixing medium in the neck of a bottle-shaped container. The mesh, having been cut with a short overlap, is rolled and slipped into position. This is needed in a narrow-necked container because of the top weight of the dried materials. These soya bean heads owe much of their attractiveness to the arched spatulate necks, but the stem is round at the base. To control the position of the stems, slit the stem end, so that it will catch in the mesh. Should your stems be too short, or should you wish to keep the soya bean dry, extend the length of the stem with a double length of wire – this will go into the mesh in the same way as the actual stem. The thin stems of the ranunculas used in this arrangement have, like those of their wild relative the buttercup, a distressing tendency to break very easily. For this reason they are cut short and supported by being placed between the fronds of asparagus plumosa. As ranunculas are long-lasting flowers, an occasional replacement of the fern will enable you to keep this arrangement for quite a long time.

17

17 This design requires the top-heavy main lily stem to stand in an upright position; the neck of the container is large enough to enable a large pinholder to be used. The thin dried vine echoes the shape of the container, and so aids the general balance of the arrangement. The ends of the vine may need to be supported in false stems – they may be too thin to fit between the needles of the pinholder, or because they soften if left in water for any length of time. The lilies have no need for special conditioning apart from a long cool drink and being cut under water. The lilac stems should be crushed, and then left in deep water to condition. All leaves that will be below the water line should be removed from the lilies. In arrangements where the lily buds are important to the general balance, a loose band of tape can be placed around their tips at night – this restriction will delay their opening. When clear glass containers are used, the visible stems should be arranged in a pattern. A pinholder would be unsightly and so a kubari of the Sogetsu type should be used. (See Introduction.)

18

18 Various techniques are used to keep materials in position in tall containers. Normally the more orthodox are the most successful for, having stood the test of years, they can be relied on and one knows exactly how much weight can be balanced and where the fixing should be placed to support it satisfactorily. Both oriental and occidental enthusiasts have their own pet theories. Occasionally, as in the arrangement shown in construction above, the materials themselves provide sufficient support. As the whole of the neck opening is to be filled it is enough to cut the ends of the main stems so that they fit snugly against the inside wall. In this way a natural cradle will be formed for the fresh branches and flowers needed to complete the arrangement. When the arrangement has been completed, and before placing it in position, give it a spray with tepid water. Do not drench it; dew is much more attractive than a downpour. In spraying take care not to damage surrounding surfaces. Gerberas are one of the few flowers that dislike being placed in deep water – their stems are covered in small hairs, and these decay rapidly under water.

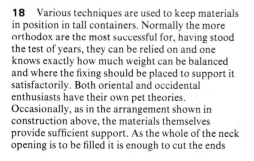

19

19 Another way of keeping materials in position in a tall vase if you have not yet mastered the kubari technique, and your stems are too soft to be pushed into oasis or too fleshy not to be damaged by wire netting, is to partially fill the container with small stones – this also gives additional weight at the base – and to place a pinholder on top of them. Calla lily stems have a habit of curling outwards after they have been in water for a time; to prevent this the bottom inch of the stem can be bound loosely with raffia. If the flower stem is particularly fat or the head heavy, further support can be given by means of a small stick. Kebab sticks are useful for this, for they are thick enough to hold a given position when they are put between the pins of an average pinholder, and yet slim enough not to fill or damage the inside of the stem. Cut your stick to the required length – two to three inches is usually long enough – and put it firmly onto the pinholder, at the angle at which you wish your flower to be. Now carefully slide the bound stem of your flower over it. A clean sharp cut is always better for stems, and especially for fleshy stems such as those of the calla lily. The faces of the flowers used here have been turned at different angles so that their full beauty of form can be enjoyed.

26

27

usec
life
have
that
next
diffe
drift
cont
have
placi
usefu
pot o
strip
this b
one o
can p
of the
troub
water
water
likely

21
the tip
mover
line o
the str

23 Experiments using tall containers co
difference being that in **23**, **24** and **25** the
the neck of the container free from materi
crossed the container from the right to the
different positions. In **23**, light bleached b
background for the more solid form of the
been taken from the stems and reassemble
in a kubari and held on the right side of the
gives a lightness to the work. Tulips seem t
flowers after they have been arranged, and
been created with them. Sugar is sometime
dip the stems into dry sugar before arrangi
stiffening effect – in this case the flowers a
solution made from one spoonful of starch

24 When few flowers are used it is bette
four especially are apt to create a balance
With many flowers it is possible to choose

26 We now leave the tall containers and concentrate on the shallow type. The arrangement made in this type of container is called a moribana style: moribana means 'piled up' flowers. In the first example you can see clearly the triangle of the occidental style – the laterals being of almost the same length as the vertical. Iris leaves have been opened and looped to form fresh green bows around the flowers. A piece of pale coral backed by a few fronds of fern has been placed at the base of the arrangement, for visual balance and to hide the pinholder.

27 On the left is a collection of good basic shapes used in modern styles of arranging. These, with one exception, would be used for natural styles – the exception being the white compote in the back row. All can have either pinholders or oasis blocks as fixing mediums. The oasis will have to be fitted into one of the special plastic holders made for it; this is then stuck to the bottom of the dish. In most European countries these styles are now being made. There are two general hazards in buying this style of container, when it has been made by a potter who has no knowledge of the use to which it will be put; sometimes they are too shallow to hold sufficient water to cover the pins of a pinholder, and they may be left in a very rough state underneath which can easily play havoc with polished surfaces.

28 In the arrangement on the right you can see the same piece of wood as used in the arrangement in **20**. On this occasion it is used in a low container, and you will be able to appreciate how much the style of container affects an arrangement.

29 Whether it is your intention to push branches into blocks of oasis or wedge them between the pins of a pinholder, it is easier if you cut the ends at an angle. You will find lines in branches easier to identify if you study the branch from the back – often you will see more beauty in a side branch than in the centre tip, especially if you leave a section of the main stem as its base. Flowers with hollow stems often present a problem of fixing since they have so little fibre to hold themselves up, and so it has become the practice, with the increased use of pinholders, to use false stems. This is excellent as long as you remember not to entirely block the channel through which the bloom must draw sustenance. If you have enough space it is often better to place your false stem on the pinholder first and then to slip the stem of the flower over it. Otherwise, handle the stem carefully as shown, and cut the false stem to the correct length before placing it in position. In this arrangement the beautiful branches of camellia have been carefully trimmed and polished prior to placing. Gerberas in lighter and darker tones than the container have been added, and to complete the arrangement two pieces of dark brown fibre have been placed around the pinholder. Water is required to come to the top of the pins of the pinholder only.

29

30

30 Prunings from old trees often have good shape, although they sometimes lack elegance. This does not, however, mean that they should be discarded, for they can be decorated. For snow scenes a little white paint or artificial snow sprayed on here or there can be very effective. Some thicker pieces can be stripped of bark and stained, and, if they have particular beauty, it may be worth the time needed to wax them. All will be more useful if stood for a day or so in some waterproof liquid, since it is most disappointing when a carefully cleaned branch is put in water and black spots of damp mould appear. There are a number of ways of fixing these pieces of dried wood for use in arrangements. You can nail them to a flat piece of board – having made the base flat and smooth so that the surfaces fit well together. For additional weight, and as a fixing medium for the other materials, a pinholder can be placed on the board – so leave enough space for it. Another method is to wedge the branch between two or three pegs which have been carefully positioned on the pinholder

to support it. Yet another idea is shown in the photograph – use a lump of clay to form a natural bank around the base of the branches, and place a pinholder near it for the other materials. Be sure that the clay you use hardens well and does not contain any substances harmful to plant life, or your flowers will be short-lived. In this landscape arrangement the three planes of nature have been incorporated; the bare branch for the distant, the pine for the middle and the sweet williams for the foreground. The rectangular container is favoured by most people for this style of arrangement. Teachers in the oriental schools advise the student to use the back of the container for the arrangement in the summer, so that a greater expanse of water can be seen and its cooling effect enjoyed. The reverse is advised for winter, for in that season one does not want to be reminded of the cold and wet. It is important when making such an arrangement in so large a container to make sure that some of the material comes forward to mask a little of its strong front line.

31

31 Gerberas, pine and leaves of the strelitzia plant have been combined in this small 'mass' arrangement. The leaves have been cut to form a fan-shaped background for the brightly coloured flowers. Although the petals of the gerberas are fine, the effect of the flower against the solid leaf is hard; for this reason a little pine has been introduced to soften the outline. The leaves of the strelitzia, incidentally, are particularly good subjects for drying by the upside-down method – that is, to hang them, in small groups, upside-down for a week or so in a warm airy place. While drying they twist and contort, and turn a pale silvery green. When absolutely dry they can be sprayed with paint, and will not soften or deteriorate. Leaves can often be made smaller by following their natural veins. In the strelitzia leaf shown you will see that they run from the centre spine to the outer edge: to reduce the leaf in size one must cut across the veins. A little cut off each day will keep the leaves fresh-looking. Leaves generally are most adaptable to change, and many different outlines can be made with them. The leaves of sansiveria, palm and flax, for instance, take quite kindly to being split down the middle and threaded through themselves. Palm can also be slit into thin fronds and rolled to make papyrus-like tassels. Study the structure of the leaf before you begin, and follow its natural form.

32

32 When choosing calla lilies look for those which have not yet produced 'snow' on their pistil: these are the younger, fresher ones. Red ixias and white lilies – arrangements using these colours are the subject of some controversy. In some countries the combination denotes happy occasions, in others it has less pleasant connotations. In this instance the lovely blue of the inside of the container can be considered part of the arrangement. The contrast in form between the two types of flowers is emphasized by the grouping, the smaller flowers having been placed high and the larger ones spread low around them. To emphasize further the colour of the inside of the container, the pinholder has been placed to the front – thus allowing the white of the lily to be seen against the blue. The ixia has a strong fibrous stem and can be cut with flower shears. Remember that the calla lily has a cellular stem which could be bruised by shears, and they should therefore be cut with a knife. This is a design for standing against a wall, so the back of it has been kept flat.

33

Strelitzia flower heads are very heavy and, if you are using a small pinholder in a container in which it is not practical to use wire mesh, the photographs show how to overcome the difficulty. Make a roll with one of the tacky adhesive materials and press it around the edge of the pinholder, put the holder into the position you have decided on, and then press the adhesive carefully so that it makes a bond between the container and the pinholder. When you are choosing strelitzia flowers, feel the pod to make sure that it is full; although the orange and blue fronds last well, each fading flower is pushed out of the back of the pod so that a new one can emerge, windmill fashion, from the front, thus giving you fresh flowers by succession for quite a long time. The blue container has been chosen to emphasize the small blue tongue of the flower. A piece of white coral has been placed at the front and at the back to cover the pinholder. Although the flowers are pointing in many directions they are all within the frame set by the container.

34

34 In all styles of arranging the longest line is measured (as shown) by the container to achieve balance. After this the length of the stems is decided by the design and visual 'weight'. In the above instance, because of its lightness, the longest material requires support – this has been afforded it not only by the addition of similar flowers but by leaving the space beneath it free. You will see that the heads of the white flowers form a triangle in themselves. Between these and the somewhat heavier heads of the sweet williams thin fronds of bleached broom act as co-ordinators. To bleach the broom is a tedious and messy business – this probably is the reason for its high cost. Should you wish to do it yourself, you will need a large container in which to boil the broom in strong bleach. When the fleshy part of the branches has softened, remove them from the bleach and hold them under running water while you brush them from base to tip with a coarse brush. When they are clean bleach them again or dye them to any colour of your choice.

35
36

35 In making the arrangements on this page a slanting character has been sought. In the upper design materials normally seen in the upright position have been shortened and used for their colours. The object has been to bring out an aspect of beauty that we do not normally recognize in these two materials. The cat-tails, or bulrushes, we are used to seeing in water, but in this design although they have been combined with another water material there is no feeling of their original forms remaining.

36 In the lower arrangement, although the lines are at the same angles as those in the one above, the character of the material lends itself to the slanting angle naturally and so the 'modern' look is not evident. The feeling of movement has been enhanced by the low, centrally placed yellow irises for these have brought the colour of the forsythia right down into the container.

37 A spiral rising from the brown depths. A twisting root starts the movement from the container, which is then continued by the shortened flower spikes of gladiolus flowers. This is a creative style arrangement, and has been designed within the line of the container.

38–40 The arrangement above is very much in the oriental style. In most schools of Japanese arrangement, the arranger is given the choice of omitting some of the main lines, or of dividing the arrangement between two or more containers or two or more pinholders in one container. The above arrangement has been divided between two pinholders placed in one container. Nerines and berried branches have been arranged with charming effect in an unusual container. On the left a collection of pairs of containers suitable for combined and divided arrangements has been assembled. A combination arrangement is one in which two or more designs are made in two or more containers, which when placed together make one whole arrangement. Unity in the materials or in the containers chosen for use is a good starting point. Take care to avoid a too balanced look. A divided arrangement is one in which the design is constructed in two separate pieces which when put together make a whole. It follows therefore that although divided arrangements can be as large as combined ones, they must be lighter for they have fewer lines in their make up. These arrangements show a strong leaning towards the oriental.

38

39

41

41   In the above photograph two containers have again been used; this time they are of similar design but different sizes. The two combined arrangements, one slightly smaller than the other, have been made with both fresh and dried materials. Many countries are now concentrating more and more on drying their natural flora; and there is now a far greater variety of material from which to make a choice. Australia, particularly, is contributing tremendously in what has hitherto been mostly a Japanese market. For convenience of transport much of the dried material is packed flat and straight and so, if you wish to bring some character to it, you must reshape it. Bending brittle material to obtain better lines can be a frustrating and, because of the damage, costly business, unless you take care to condition it first. According to the type and thickness of the stem, softening should be done by immersing it in warm water and then carefully bending it. The dried pines of a palm leaf are shown being brought from the straight to a winding, willowy curve.

42   In the divided arrangement shown on the right, four gladioli have been used. These have been carefully trimmed and graded. The flower used for the longest line has been left intact, those for the second and third lines have been shortened

from the top – the cut having been made just above the lowest green buds. The fourth flower has been cut into three sections and placed in a separate group on the right side of the container. All the leaves have been placed in the larger group. Dark stones have been used to cover the kenzan, so that the impact of the contrast between the brilliant red flowers and the high gloss container has not been lost. With fewer flowers of a less vibrant hue, the arranger could with quite pleasing effect use a gnarled piece of driftwood to form a bridge between the two groups. Arrangements made with heavy flowers are sometimes difficult to balance on small pinholders since the ever-changing character, as the flowers develop, may require the position to be changed and one does not always want to resort to adhesives. The triangle of placement recommended in the Japanese schools is very helpful, and often a heavy flower inclining slightly to the back will act as a counter-balance to those brought forward. A little more emphasis placed on this line to the back turns an arrangement into one of great depth, which is often needed to give accent to a corner position. The direction in which the actual blooms face on the gladioli stems can be changed by gentle persuasion. With one hand hold them firmly but gently at the base and with the other stroke them onto the other side of the stem.

43 We now progress from using two containers to making a composition using several. In this instance one arrangement has been divided and placed in three of a group of four containers. The containers are the same colour, but contrasting in shape. One stem of lily flowers has been used, which has been divided in a manner not unlike that used for the gladioli on the previous page. The individual beauty of this flower is often lost when it is used in a mass arrangement, as one cannot appreciate its regal and translucent beauty to the

full extent. By separating the stem and isolating the flowers and buds, their individual beauty has been brought to the fore. One difficulty to be faced when separating a flower which produces all its flower heads from one point, is the shortness of most of the stems. High and low containers obviously overcome this. Pinholders have been used as fixing mediums in the shorter containers, and a short length of stick in the taller one. The natural coronet of leaves has been left as a feature of the taller arrangement – the shorter ones rely on simplicity.

43

44 In Japanese, arrangements made in these tall containers are called nageire, which means 'thrown in' style. The history of its development we have discussed in our introduction. As with so many oriental things, colourful legend also surrounds it. One story of its origin tells of warriors resting between battles who sought relaxation and entertainment by arranging flowers – this was a manly occupation and a recognized art. No containers were available and so the arrangement of a few wild irises and leaves was bound to a knife and 'thrown' – the knife sticking into the ground on landing provided the support for the flowers. Another story relates that the sister of a prince found the heavy branches required for the rikkwa arrangements too heavy for her, for she was very petite, and so she made smaller arrangements to her own design – these were considered beautiful but when compared with the regal rikkwa styles were almost casual, and so the term 'thrown in' was attached to them. Whatever the reason for the name, the fact remains that these arrangements made in tall containers are expected to be natural in style, and modern arrangements are not often made in them. When designing, consideration should be given to the direction from which the light comes for the lines look much better if placed to 'receive light'. In old tokonomas, the recesses built into the Japanese homes for arrangements and treasures, the light came from one side, and the higher side of the arrangement received the light. All the old classical arrangements were designed with this in mind, and conformed to the hongatte style (lines curved to the left) or the gyakugatte (curved to the right). The greatest difficulty one finds in the nageire style of arranging is the retention of space – in ikebana arrangements one is expected to leave three-quarters of the neck opening of the container free; this rules out the use of wire netting, oasis and such aids, for they are unsightly and must be covered. Kubaris are used for convenience, and achieve a better style. The kubari is a device made from one

or two sticks placed at a relevant point to keep the materials in the correct position. The gladioli in the arrangement on the left have been secured thus, and you will see that a large section of the neck of the container remains clear.

45 The iris is regarded in Japan as one of the more important flowers. It is used for a festival held on the fifth day of the fifth month. Paper models of carp are flown from poles outside the homes in which there are sons. It is a national birthday for boys in which all Japanese families give thanks for the birth of sons, and express the hope that they will grow up to be forthright and strong citizens to bear the sword with courage for the honour of family and country. The iris leaf is thought to be reminiscent of the sword in shape, and it is possibly for this reason that the flower was chosen. The iris used as the festival flower is iris ensata (elegant spirit) which is not widely grown in Europe. As the flowers are very short-lived, conditioning is very important, and it is advisable to cut the stems under water, to dip the cut end into dry salt and then to lay them horizontally for two or three minutes before arranging them. The design featured above is called the 'fish path' – it is characteristic of this arrangement that space is left between the groups of flowers, so that the fish are free to swim between them and enjoy the flowers also. A smaller group is always placed to the rear to add perspective. In flat containers, when two or three groups are used, care should be taken to see that no line joining two pinholders is parallel to the front of the container. Each group has a drift of small stones around the pinholder to help to obscure it, and to add to the water landscape image of the arrangement. Incidentally white stones denote water and black stones land. Both blue and white colours are used to represent water, as well as water plants. No particular colour of flower represents land, although land plants would obviously be chosen for landscape.

46

46–47 Every hobby has its tools and flower arranging is no exception. Photographed above are some of those recommended by the arranger of these designs. From left to right, starting at the top left corner, there is an atomiser – this is invaluable for spraying the finished arrangement and keeping it fresh. Many plants absorb moisture through their leaves. Next is a block of oasis – this is an absorbent material which retains water, and is firm enough to hold most flowers and branches in position; it can be cut to fit into any container. This material is available under a number of trade names and in many shapes, and sometimes has flower food incorporated in it. The only warning about this is that some flowers wilt when placed in it. Plastic covered wire netting is shown next: this is easy to roll for holding materials in slim-necked containers. Common chicken wire, which is rust proof, is a great standby for many

arrangers of the occidental styles. The small can with the long spout is of immense help when topping up the water in arrangements – the water should be kept within half an inch of the top of the container. A finger held over the rim when you are filling up will give enough warning to prevent flooding. In the lower line are clay and adhesive, marbles for filling up glass containers, scissors and a selection of tapes sometimes used for repairing broken stems. Below is a selection of containers suitable for modern work.

48 On this page is shown one of the containers in **47**. This has been sprayed dark blue, as have the dried branches of mitsumata, and combined with pale-coloured straw flowers to make an interesting mass and line arrangement quite different from the usual style of dried designs.

47

49

49 A cycas leaf, stripped on one side and twisted into a shape similar to that of the container in which it has been placed, is the dominant feature of this design. As most of these leaves have short stems, they are easier to arrange if you lengthen them. This is done by splitting and interlocking the end with an additional piece of thin branch and then wiring the two together. Many different effects can be obtained by spraying these dried leaves with paint. When they are quite dry, experiment by arranging them with various fresh and dried flowers and leaves – quite unusual and amusing results can be obtained. For the Christmas season

brilliant red ranunculas and glossy green camellia leaves have been used. All these materials are long-lasting. Overcome the weakness of the ranunculas, the easily broken stem, by using it short and supported by other materials, and you have an arrangement which can be made in advance and which will last.

50 Branches of acacia spinosa have been stripped and arranged in a natural way with small roses. The material in this design has been deliberately understated to emphasize the beauty of the pestle and mortar.

51

51 In the above design you will see that the traditional combination of pine and roses has been used as a supplement to the gay swinging circles of split bamboo. These circles can also be made from round and flat cane of various thicknesses. Soak the selected material in tepid water until it is supple, form a circle – working from the inside to the out – round your finger or hand holding one side of it close together. Fasten the closed side with a small tack and then tie firmly with raffia. When the material is absolutely dry the circles will be set and the tie can then be removed. As well as giving a feeling of gaiety, circles can convey messages. The recurring circles used above can mean, on the occasion of a birthday, 'many happy returns', recurring good wishes. Because of the full nature of the design, oasis has been used as a fixing medium. Cut a section from the main block which is slightly larger than the container opening, and being careful to keep it vertical push it gently into position – the excess will be cut away from the rim and the rest remain firmly wedged. Before making the arrangement immerse the container in water until the air bubbles from the oasis have stopped rising to the surface – this is indicative of saturation. In a container with such a small neck it would be messy to soak the oasis prior to insertion, and probably cause it to crumble.

52–54 These arrangements continue to use material entirely for form and colour. Knowledge of the recessive qualities of colour will be of great help in this phase of arranging; the occidental arranger will possibly have received more training in this than the student of the oriental style. The greater the variety of flowers and colour used in one arrangement, the greater is the need for visual balance. The student of ikebana will have concentrated more on line and placement to achieve the required effect. The lucky person who has found time to study both aspects will be well equipped. In the above arrangement, red flowers in a slanting position have been placed in a strong round container. The round seed heads of the lotus have been added to complement it. In old times red flowers were not used by themselves in Japanese arrangements because they remind one of fire, and this is a very real fear for the people who lived in easily inflammable houses. If for some reason red flowers had to be used, then one was obliged to add some white – for the water. The use of a

slanting line with this shaped container means that it is not practical to use a pinholder as a fixing medium. A short piece of stick tied at right angles across the ends of the stems will prevent the flowers from turning. The two white stones are important accessories. The gladioli spurs have been shortened to a bud showing colour.

The arrangements shown on the following pages are creative works. Flower arranging is an art to be shared between the arranger and the viewer. People have very individual ideas of fantasy and interpretation – what to one person looks like a bird, to another can be a contour of a mountain. What to one looks sad gives another a feeling of tranquillity. In the arrangement using white prunus and iris, one person saw the outline of a butterfly; another was reminded of a young girl at her wedding. To give a title to an arrangement might restrict the imagination of the viewer. For instance in **54**, pink gladioli, asparagus fern, and fine feathers – what thoughts do they evoke in you?

55

55 This arrangement has an interesting form and a minimum of colour. We have spoken of messages and meanings conveyed through the type of plant; we know that there is a language of colour; we know that straight lines are masculine and curves feminine. Sometimes sheer design can in itself be sufficient – the combination of segments of a circle with vertical and horizontal lines is an interesting exercise. Try with fresh pussy willow wands or with green bloom, and stand straight iris flowers or mini-ixias amongst them.

56 This is an excellent example of visual and physical balance. Top-heavy materials have been arranged in a comparatively small compote. Strelitzia heads have been turned in different directions to spread the weight. Long cones of pine have been placed at the front and back, as have pine branches.

58

59

57   The last arrangement, before we proceed to those made by a grand master of one of the most famous schools of ikebana in Japan, is a simple one from all aspects. The container is one which could be in daily use, and the flowering materials simple – irises and peach blossom. It is the beauty of nature which makes flower arranging such an attractive and satisfying art.

58–59   The two arrangements on this page, and those that follow, are creations of the Japanese master Houn Ohara, made for an important exhibition of Japanese art in Milan. This exhibition was an unusual one and was of particular interest to ikebana enthusiasts, who very rarely get the chance to see the work of great Japanese masters. The arrangement on the left was done by Houn Ohara for the Girls' Festival, which, as we have said, is celebrated in Japan on 3rd March. The master included in his design the branches of the

peach tree, which represent feminine grace and adolescence. The other elements of the arrangement are light and flexible shoots of weeping willow, which, twisted here and there into the shape of a nest, symbolize long life, and make one think also of young girls; some fresh and delicate camellias; and some pieces of dry wood, which, artistically arranged, form the structural base of the composition. The other masterpiece, **59**, represents the awakening of nature in the spring; it is made up of branches of forsythia, dried bleached palm leaves, bamboo, and strange and interesting fan shapes made of coloured card. The whole, in an eccentric modern vase, is a poetic fantasy.

The Japanese do not only love flowers in arrangements: they also like to see them in full bloom in their natural state. The cherry tree in particular is very popular, and every year people come from all over Japan to see the ancient cherry orchards in their spring glory.

61

60　Stripped branches, arranged in an artistic tangle, represent the snow 'which moves on the mountains'. This sculptural modern composition is livened up and completed by elegant strelitzia, original pieces of coloured card, and various pieces of greenery. All this material is grouped into the centre and gives an air of solidity to the whole, while the upper part remains light and almost frothy. The ceramic container has a very small base, but the arrangement is so well balanced that it is quite stable.

61　In an exceptionally large container, here is an enormous arrangement made with great branches and sprigs of camellia. The overall effect, despite the unusual size, is of excellent proportion and beautiful elegance, thanks to the mastery and experience of the arranger. We must point out here that apart from the 'domestic ikebana' which is used to decorate the home and is therefore usually quite small, there is also 'exhibition ikebana'. This aspect of the art has

arisen from the need to decorate the cold bare rooms in which exhibitions are usually held, with conspicuous flower arrangements – which would of course have to be proportionate to the size of the rooms. The arrangement above, in its extraordinary vase which is a copy of an ancient Japanese terracotta vase, is a typical example of 'exhibition ikebana'. The large branches form a sort of scaffolding, and they are fixed together with a large number of nails. Of course these arrangements take a long time to do, and often the masters of ikebana simply draw the design and then leave the practical execution of the arrangement to a team of workers.

62　In this unusual ceramic vase with two mouths is an arrangement of twigs of edgeworthia, pineapple and dried fronds of bracken. The twigs are used upside-down, according to a widespread custom among Japanese masters, who know a thousand secrets for making the best use of all the materials they have.